ISBN: 978-1-0915645-5-8

Copyright © 2019 by Black Girl Magic - All Rights Reserved.

All Rights Reserved. Except as permitted under the U.S. Copyright Act of 1976, no part of this publication may be reproduced, distributed, or transmitted in any form or by any means, or stored in a database or retrieval system, without the prior written permission of the publisher.

Written & Created by Mia Harris
Published by Basik Studios • Design & Layout by Michael Matulka
Illustrations by Tiffany Wilson • Color Art by Angela Kluesner

Printed in the United States of America

B

Believe
(Always Believe In Yourself)

> Write Like ....Marley
> Speak Like .... Yari
> Shine Like..............Serena
> Dance Like.............. Misty
> Fierce Like ....Simone
> Lead Like.............. Marsai

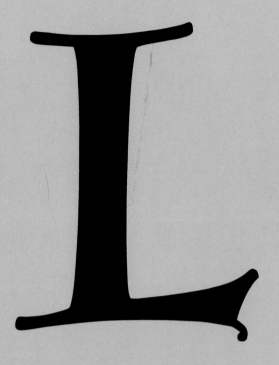

Leadership
(Always Lead, Never Follow)

" Black Girl from the top of your
Fro to the tip of your Toe! "

Apply Yourself
(Always Apply Yourself)

" Little Miss Magic be who You are! "

C

Confidence
(Always Be Confident)

66 Black Girls will always ROCK! 99

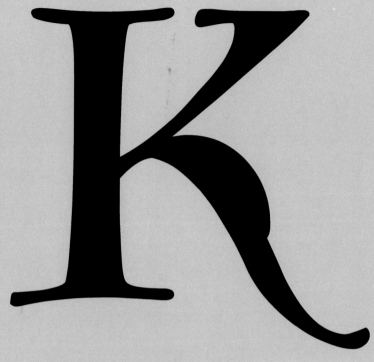

Knowledge
(Always Be Knowledgeable)

❝ Magical Since you were born! ❞

Genuine
(Always Be Your Genuine Self)

" Little Princess's with Dreams,
become Queens's with a Vision! "

Inspiration
(Always Be Inspirational)

66 You have the Strength and Power of a million moons! **99**

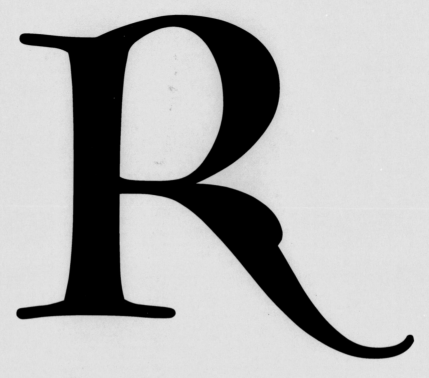

Resilientcy
(Always Be Resilient)

" Don't be Afraid of Your Shade! "

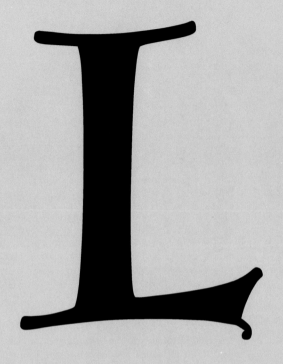

Love Yourself
(Always Love Yourself)

" Spread your kindness
around like Confetti! "

M

Motivation
(Always Be Motivated)

" Black Girl, You create pixie dust so that makes You Magical! "

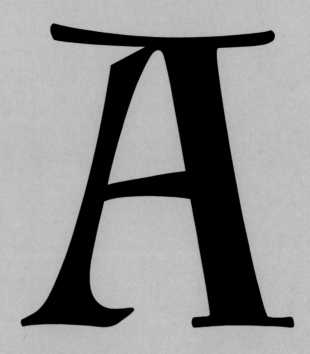

Authenticity
(Always Be Your Authentic Self)

" You have Black Girl Magic in Your veins! **"**

Goal Setter
(Always Set Your Goals)

" You are... "

Pretty Enough
Smart Enough
Strong Enough

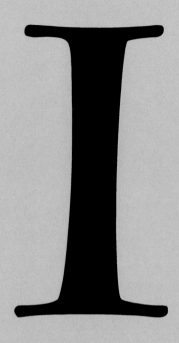

Individuality
(Always Be Your Individual Self)

" Always leave a little sparkle and glitter everywhere you go! **"**

Courageous
(Be Courageous In Everything You Do)

" May your Hair Grow
and your Skin Glow! "

Copyright © 2019 by Black Girl Magic - All Rights Reserved.

43037847R00018

Made in the USA
Middletown, DE
19 April 2019

The Grandma Book

TODD PARR

W9-BRX-318

Megan Tingley Books
LITTLE, BROWN AND COMPANY
New York Boston

Todd Parr is the author of more than thirty books
for children, including the *New York Times* bestselling
The I Love You Book, The Earth Book, and *The Thankful Book.*
He lives in Berkeley, California.

Also by Todd Parr:

It's Okay to Be Different
The Peace Book
We Belong Together
The I'm Not Scared Book
The Feelings Book
The Feel Good Book

The Mommy Book
The Daddy Book
The Grandpa Book
The Family Book
Reading Makes You Feel Good
Otto Goes to School

A complete list of
Todd's books and more information, can be found at
www.toddparr.com.

Copyright © 2006 by Todd Parr

All rights reserved. In accordance with the U.S. Copyright Act of 1976, the scanning, uploading, and electronic sharing of any part of this book without the permission of the publisher is unlawful piracy and theft of the author's intellectual property. If you would like to use material from the book (other than for review purposes), prior written permission must be obtained by contacting the publisher at permissions@hbgusa.com. Thank you for your support of the author's rights.

Little, Brown and Company • Hachette Book Group • 1290 Avenue of the Americas, New York, NY 10104 • Visit our website at www.lb-kids.com

Little, Brown and Company is a division of Hachette Book Group, Inc. • The Little, Brown name and logo are trademarks of Hachette Book Group, Inc.

The publisher is not responsible for websites (or their content) that are not owned by the publisher.

First Paperback Edition: April 2011
First published in hardcover in April 2006 by Little, Brown and Company

Library of Congress Cataloging-in-Publication Data
Parr, Todd.
The grandma book / by Todd Parr. — 1st ed.
p. cm.
"Megan Tingley Books"
Summary: Presents the different ways grandmothers show their
grandchildren love, from offering advice and babysitting to making things and giving lots of kisses.
ISBN 978-0-316-05802-5 (hc) / ISBN 978-0-316-07041-6 (pb)
[1. Grandmothers—Fiction. 2. Grandparent and child—Fiction.] I. Title.
PZ7.P2447Gr 2006
[E]—dc22   2004027846

10 9 8 7
IM
Printed in China

This book is dedicated to my Grandma Parr. Some of my fondest memories are of her baking and her special cookie drawer. But my fondest memories of all are of the Christmas gifts of underwear and socks, which were at least five sizes too big.

And to my Grandma Logan, who has always been such a big part of my life. We talk every Sunday and she gives me ladybugs for good luck. Thanks for always being there for me and believing in me even when I didn't believe in myself. Thanks for reading GREEN EGGS AND HAM, over and over and over.

I love you very much.
Love,
Todd

Some grandmas have a lot of cats

Some grandmas have a lot of purses

Some grandmas give you a lot of advice

Some grandmas give you a lot of books

All grandmas are happy

when you spend the night

Some grandmas help their neighbors

Some grandmas help take care of their grandchildren

Some grandmas like to make you eat a lot

Some grandmas like to
make you things

All grandmas like to

hear from you

Some grandmas like to dance

Some grandmas like to play bingo

Some grandmas live with a grandpa

Some grandmas live with their friends

Some grandmas drive slowly

Some grandmas drive fast

All grandmas like to

give you lots of kisses

Grandmas are very special! They make sure you are warm and safe and that you always have a full tummy. They know everything! Tell them you love them every day. ♡ Love, Todd